TOM WAITS
ANTHOLOGY

MW01042836

Amsco Publications
New York/London/Sydney/Cologne

Front cover photo by A.J. Barratt/Retna Ltd.
Back cover photo by Patrick Quigley/Retna Ltd.
Interior photos by Ebet Roberts, Santo Basone/Retna Ltd., and Elaine Bryant/Retna Ltd.

This book Copyright © 1988 by Amsco Publications,
A Division of Music Sales Corporation, New York, NY.

US International Standard Book Number: 0.8256.2503.3
UK International Standard Book Number: 0.7119.1486.9
Order No. AM 71168

Exclusive Distributors:
Music Sales Corporation
225 Park Avenue South, New York, NY 10003, USA
Music Sales Limited
8/9 Frith Street, London W1V 5TZ England
Music Sales Pty. Limited
120 Rothschild Street, Rosebery, Sydney, NSW 2018, Australia

Printed in the United States of America by
Vicks Lithograph and Printing Corporation

(Looking for) The Heart of Saturday Night

Words and Music by
Tom Waits

Well, you gassed her___ up.   Be-hind the___ wheel   with your

6

9

Ghosts of Saturday Night
(After Hours at Napoleone's Pizza House)

Words and Music by
Tom Waits

Slow Blues
(Background under recitation, play 4 times)

Recitation

1. A cab combs the snake,
   Tryin' to rake in that last night's fare,
   And a solitary sailor
   Who spends the facts of his life small change on strangers ...

2. Paws his inside P-coat pocket for a welcome twenty-five cents,
   And the last bent butt from a package of Kents,
   As he dreams of a waitress with Maxwell House eyes
   And marmalade things with scrambled yellow hair.

3. Her rhinestone-studded moniker says, "Irene"
   As she wipes the wisps of dishwater blond from her eyes.

4. And Texaco beacon burns on,
   The steel-belted attendant with a 'Ring and Valve Special' ...
   Cryin' "Fill 'er up" and check that oil,
   "You know it could be a distributor and it could be a coil."

5. The early mornin' final edition's on the stands,
   That town cryer's cryin' there with nickels in his hands.
   Pigs in a blanket sixty-nine cents,
   Eggs - roll 'em over and a package of Kents,
   Adam and Eve on a log, you can sink 'em damn straight,
   Hash browns, hash browns, you know I can't be late.

6. And an early dawn cracks out a carpet of diamond
   Across a cash crop car lot filled with twilight Coupe Devilles,
   Leaving the town in a-keeping
   Of the one who is sweeping

   Up the ghost of Saturday night ...

Burma Shave

Words and Music by
Tom Waits

Quite freely (rubato)

1. Lic - 'rice ta - too turned a gun met - al blue, —

Scrawled a - cross the shoul - ders of the dy - ing town. Took the

nick - el's worth of dreams and ev - 'ry wish - bone that they saved Lie

swin - dled from them on the way to Bur - ma

Shave. _____ 6. And the

sun hit the der - rick and cast a bat - wing sha - dow

Tom Traubert's Blues
(Four Sheets to the Wind in Copenhagen)

Words and Music by
Tom Waits

Verses:

5. No, I don't want your sympathy,
   The fugitives say the streets arent for dreaming now.
   Manslaughter dragnets and the ghosts that sell memories,
   They want a piece of the action anyhow. Go . . . *(Chorus)*

6. And you can ask any sailor,
   And the keys from the jailer,
   And the old men in wheelchairs know
   That Matilda's the defendant, and she killed about a hundred,
   And she follows wherever you may go. *(Chorus)*

(𝄋)7. And it's a battered old suitcase to a hotel some place,
   And a wound that will never heal.
   No prima donna, the perfume is on an old (shirt . . . *etc.*) *To Coda*

Jersey Girl

Words and Music by
Tom Waits

Ol' 55

Words and Music by
Tom Waits

Heartattack and Vine

Words and Music by
Tom Waits

I Wish I Was in New Orleans
(In the Ninth Ward)

Words and Music by
Tom Waits

Well, I wish I was in New Or- leans, I can see it in my dreams.

3. And deal the cards, roll the dice.
If it ain't that ole Chuck E. Weiss.
And Clayborn Avenue, me and you,
Sam Jones and all.
And I wish I was in New Orleans,
I can see it in my dreams.
Arm in arm down Burgundy,
A bottle and my friends and me,
New Orleans I'll be there.

Annie's Back in Town

Words and Music by
Tom Waits

Old Boyfriends

Words and Music by
Tom Waits

Old boy - friends, lost in the pock - et of your o - ver-coat, like burned out light - bulbs on a fer - ris wheel.

2. Old boyfriends,
   Remember when you were burning for them?
   Why do you keep turning them into
   Old boyfriends?
   They look you up when they're in town,
   To see if they can still burn you down.
   You fell in love, you see . . . *(etc.)*

3. Old boyfriends
   Turn up every time it rains,
   Fall out of the pages in a magazine.
   Old boyfriends.
   Girls fill up the bars every spring,
   Not places for remembering. *(To Coda)*

On the Nickel

Words and Music by
Tom Waits

60

62

63

Shiver Me Timbers

Words and Music by
Tom Waits

1. I'm leav - in' my___ fam'-ly,   leav - in' all ___ my_ friends.
2. And I know Mar - tin E - den   is gon - na be proud of__ me,
3. So please call my___ mis-sus   and tell her not ___ to_ cry,

My bod - y's at home___   but, my heart's in the wind. Where the
and man - y be - fore me   who've been called by the sea. To be
'cause my good-bye is writ - ten   by the moon in the sky. Hey and

Martha

Words and Music by
Tom Waits

I Never Talk to Strangers

Words and Music by
Tom Waits

Kentucky Avenue

Words and Music by
Tom Waits

2. And we'll break all the windows in the old Anderson place,
   We'll steal a bunch of boysenberries and I'll smear 'em on your face.

3. I'll get a dollar from my mama's purse and buy that skull-and-crossbones ring,
   And you can wear it around your neck on an old piece of string.

4. Then we'll spit on Ronnie Arnold and flip him the bird,
   And slash the tires on the school bus, now don't say a word.

5. I'll take a rusty nail and scratch your initials in my arm,
   I'll show you how to sneak up on the roof of the drugstore.

6. I'll take the spokes from your wheelchair and a magpie's wings,
   And I'll tie 'em to your shoulders and your feet.

7. I'll steal a hacksaw from my dad and cut the braces off your legs,
   And we'll bury them tonight out in the cornfield.

8. Just put a church key in your pocket ... (etc.)

Take Me Home

Words and Music by
Tom Waits

San Diego Serenade

Words and Music by
Tom Waits

Red Shoes by the Drugstore

Words and Music by
Tom Waits

Steady moving beat

No Chord

(quasi 'sing - talk' throughout)

1. She wore Red

shoes   by the news-stand   as the rain___ splashed the nick - le

and spilled like chab - lis   all a - long the mid-way.___   There's a lit - tle

bus stop, um-brel-las ar-ranged in a sad bou-quet. Lit-tle

Ce-sar got caught, he's go-in' on down a sec-ond, He was cooled chang-in'

sta-tions on the cham-ber to steal a dia-mond ring from a jew'l-ry

store for his ba-by. He loved the way she looked in those Red

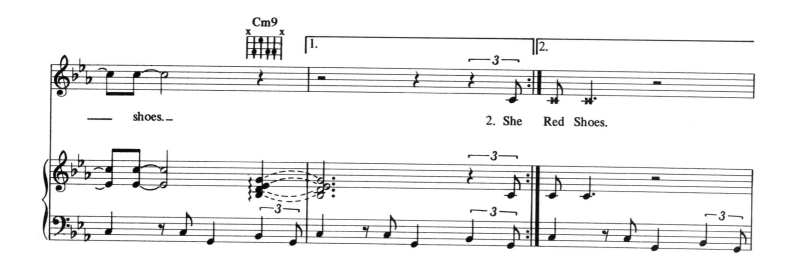

shoes. — 2. She Red Shoes.

Repeat and fade

Wear your Red Shoes.

2. She waited by the drugstore,
   Caesar'd never been this late before.
   Dogs bayed the moon and rattled their chains,
   And the cold jingle of taps in a puddle
   Was the burglar alarm snitchin' on Caesar.
   And the rain washes memories from sidewalks,
   And the hounds splash the nickel full of soldiers.
   Santa Claus is drunk in the sky room,
   And it's Christmas Eve in a sad cafe.
   When the moon gets its way,
   There's a little blue jay by the newsstand,
   With red shoes, wearin' red shoes.
   So meet me tonight by the drugstore,
   Meet me tonight by the drugstore,
   Meet me tonight by the drugstore.
   We're goin' out tonight,
   We're goin' out tonight,
   Goin' out tonight.
   Wear your Red Shoes,
   Red Shoes . . .
   Red Shoes . . .
   Red Shoes . . .

Christmas Card from a Hooker in Minneapolis

Words and Music by
Tom Waits

Hey, Char-lie, I'm preg-nant, liv-in' on Ninth Street, _____

Right a-bove the dirt-y book-store _____ off Euc-lid Av-e-nue. _____

A Sight for Sore Eyes

Words and Music by
Tom Waits

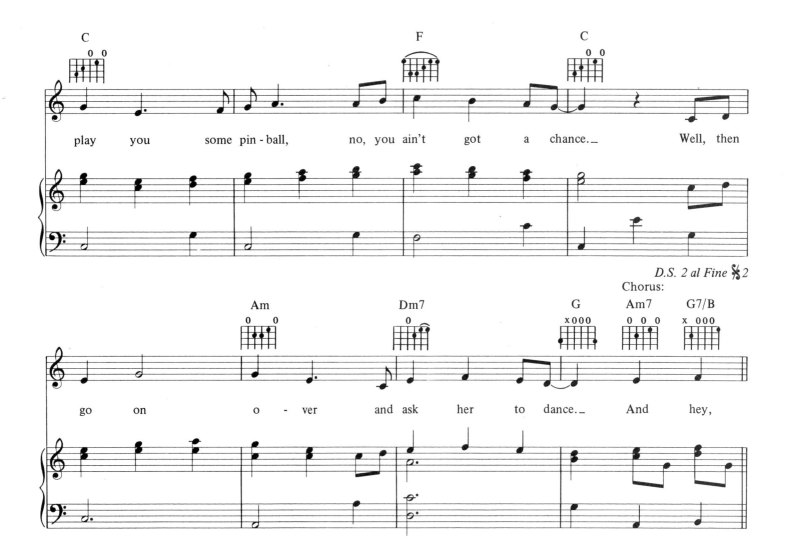

play you some pin-ball, no, you ain't got a chance._ Well, then

D.S. 2 al Fine 𝄋 2

Chorus:

go on o-ver and ask her to dance._ And hey,

2.No, the old gang ain't around, everyone has left town,
  'Cept for Thumm and Giardina, said they just might be down.
  Oh, half drunk all the time, and I'm all drunk the rest,
  Yeah, Monk's still the champion, oh, but I am the best. *(To Chorus)*

3.I guess you heard about Nash, he was killed in a crash,
  That must 've been two or three years ago now.
  Yeah he spun out and he rolled, he hit a telephone pole,
  And he died with the radio on. *(To Coda)*

Ruby's Arms

Words and Music by
Tom Waits

106

New Coat of Paint

Words and Music by
Tom Waits

You wear a dress,__ ba-by, I'll wear a tie._____ We'll laugh at that old, blood-shot moon__ in that bur-gun-dy sky.__

2nd Verse

All our scribbled love dreams are lost or thrown away,
Here amidst the shuffle of an overflowin' day.
Our love needs a transfusion so let's shoot it full of wine.
Fishin' for a good time starts with throwin' in your line.

Blue Valentines

Words and Music by
Tom Waits

2. Blue valentines, like half - forgotten dreams,
Like a pebble in my shoe as I walk these streets,
And the ghost of your memory
Baby, there's a sizzle in the kiss,
It's the burglar that can break a rose's neck,
It's the tatooed broken promise.
I got eyes beneath my sleeve,
I'm gonna see you every time I turn my back.

3. You send me blue valentines, though I try to remain at large,
They're insisting that our love must have a eulogy.
Why do I save all this madness here in the nightstand drawer,
There to haunt upon my shoulders, baby, I know
I'd be luckier to walk around everywhere I go
With this blind and broken heart that sleeps beneath my lapel,
Instead these . . .

4. Blue valentines to remind me of my cardinal sin,
I can never wash the guilt or get these bloodstains off my hands,
And it takes a lot of whiskey to make these nightmares go away.
And I cut my bleeding heart out every night,
And I'm gonna die just a little more
On each Saint Valentine's Day.
Don't you remember, I promised I would write you
These blue valentines, blue valentines,
Blue valentines.

Broken Bicycles

Words and Music by
Tom Waits

Semi Suite

Words and Music by
Tom Waits

stop - pin' when he can.   He's a truck driv - in' man, __   stop - pin' when he

can.

2. But the curtain - laced billow,
   And his hands on your pillow,
   And his trousers are hangin' on the chair.

   You're lyin' through your pain, babe,
   But you're gonna tell him he's your man,
   And you ain't got the courage to leave.

3. He tells you that you're on his mind,
   You're the only one he's ever gonna find
   That's kind-a special, understands his complicated soul . . .

   The only place a man can breath
   And collect his thoughts
   Midnight and flyin' away on the road.

4. That you've packed and unpacked
   So many times you've lost track,
   And the steam heat is drippin' off the walls.

   But when you hear his engines,
   You're lookin' throught the window in the kitchen and you knew
   You're always gonna be there when he calls,

   'Cause he's a truck drivin' man, stoppin' when he can,
   He's a truck drivin' man, stoppin' when he can.

'Til the Money Runs Out

Words and Music by
Tom Waits

2. Can't you hear the thunder, someone stole my watch,
   I sold a quart of blood and bought a half a pint of scotch.
   Someone tell those Chinamen on Telegraph Canyon Road:
   When you're on the bill with the spoon, there ain't no time to unload,
   So bye bye, baby; baby, bye bye.

3. Droopy stranger, lonely dreamer, toy puppy on the Prado,
   We're laughin' as they piled into Olmo's El Dorado.
   Jesus, whispered eenie meenie meenie minie moe
   They're too pround to duck their heads, that's why they bring it down so low.

4. The pointed man is smack dab in the middle of July,
   Swingin' from the rafters in his brand new tie.
   He said, "I can't go back to that hotel room . . . all they do is shout,
   But I'll stay wichew, baby, 'till the money runs out!"
   So bye bye, baby; baby, bye bye.

5. Strange bev'rage that falls out from the sky,
   Splashin' Bagdad on the Hudson in Panther Martin's eyes.
   He's high and outside wearin' candy apple red,
   Scarlet gave him twenty-seven stitches in his head.
   With a pint of green chartreuse, ain't nothin' seems right,
   You buy the Sunday paper on Saturday night.
   Bye bye, baby; baby, bye bye.

This One's from the Heart

Words and Music by
Tom Waits

Invitation to the Blues

Words and Music by
Tom Waits

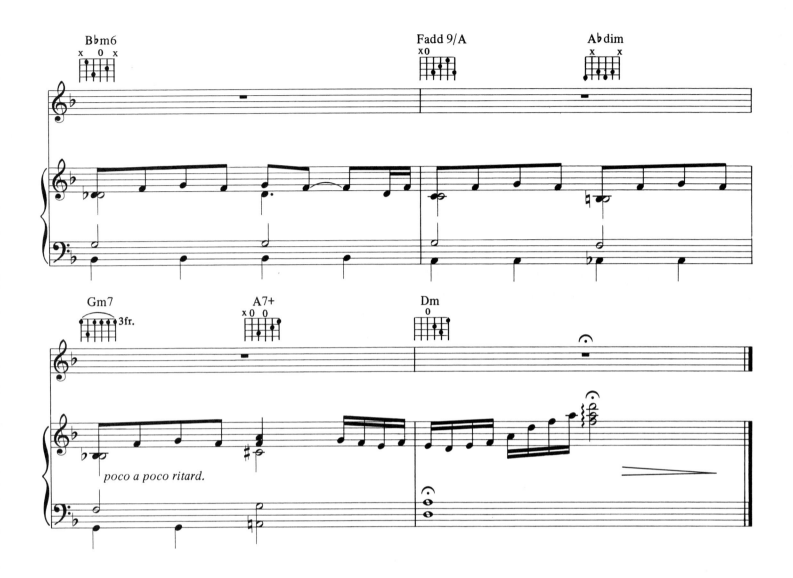

3. But she used to have a sugar daddy,
   And a candyapple caddy,
   And a bank account and everything
   Accostumed to the finer things.
   He probably left her for a socialite,
   He didn't love her 'cept at night,
   And then he's drunk and never told her that he cared.

   So they took the registration,
   The car keys and his shoes,
   And left with invitation to the blues.

4. But there's a Continental Trailways leavin',
   Local bus tonight, good evening,
   You can have my seat,
   I'm stickin' 'round here for a while,
   Get me a room at the Dquire.
   The fillin' station's hiring,
   Now I can eat here everynight, what the hell have I got to lose.

   Got a crazy sensation,
   Go or stay, and I gotta choose,
   And I'll accept your invitation to the blues.

Foreign Affair

Words and Music by
Tom Waits

bonds I knowed_ don't ev - er want to find the cul - prit that re - mains the ob - ject of their long re -

lent - less quest. The ob - ses - sion's in the chas - ing and not the ap - pre - hend - ing, the pur -

suit, you see, and nev - er the ar - rest. With - out

fear of con - tra - dic - tion, "bon voy - age" is al - ways hol - lered_ in con - junc - tion with a hand - ker - chief from